Dawn of
My Next Decade

Dawn of
My Next Decade

Talia McClure-Moore

Library of Congress Control Number: 2010917441
ISBN: Softcover   978-1-4568-2055-8
                               Ebook   978-1-4568-2056-5

This book was printed in the United States of America.

To order additional copies of this book, contact:
Xlibris Corporation
1-888-795-4274
www.Xlibris.com
Orders@Xlibris.com
86145

Contents

Life is a Contradiction

Death and taxes are certain,
every thing else is gray matter.
Highs, lows, good times and bad;
tears and laughter.
Good girls gone bad;
bad boys turned good.
From the projects to the Palisades;
Melrose to the hood.
Republican but liberal;
a conservative democrat.
Social services to aid the poor.
The rich not in support of that.
America yet a nation divided
Thirteen stars to fifty states.
Poor people can't afford to live
Healthcare debate.
Pro athletes breaking records
Steroids flow in their bloodstream.
Loved and adored by the fans
Black-balled by the team.
Light-skin, red-bone, mulatto, creole
Good hair; nap free
Tragic mulatto, master's mistress, house nigga
Jigga boo or wanna be.
Curvaceous frame, full lips, thick thighs
Camels hump on lower back.
Big-boned, over weight, high blood pressure
Conventionally fat.
The working poor, middle lower class, blue collar
The meat and potatoes of this great nation.
X, Y or Baby Boomer
Labels placed on your generation.

A democratic majority kudos and cheers
when this changing of the guards took place.
Yet no real resolutions, changes, upgrades
or new law mandates.
A toothless smile, a cheesy grin, dancing eyes,
closed bark and no bite.
Fist unclenched, cowering to defeat
a weakling antagonizing a fight.
Disliking your man or your momma
but still loving them unconditionally.
Lifting weights daily, over hauling an entire car
But being off on disability.
What should be has become
A set of self imposed contradictions.
No more real or more fake
Than folklore or superstitions.
To hear it means one thing and seeing it
has a reality at its polar opposite end.
The chicken or egg; which came first?
Both arguments you can defend.
In reality I eat both so please
Just ensure they meet my plate.
I know what time it starts
But regardless I'll be arriving late.
To try hard and study
But still continue to fail.
Stop caring puff, puff pass the test
Above I sail.
Struggle and success go hand in hand
My reality to bare.
Life is a contradiction
My secret that to you I share.

T-Day Turmoil

It's funny how perception is reality, at least to the one who perceives.

Despite the presence of an alternate truth, one which is hard to receive.

Looked at by many as the family's golden child with a couple of degrees.

Yet as a child with short hair and dark skin, I was regarded more as a disease.

Tables now turned and facts and fiction interwoven, blended over time.

Your reality versuses my perception; your perception and facts and reality of mine.

How easy we forget who really had it good as a child.

My daddy in your momma's house and me with ole' crazy all the while.

Silver spoons no, that was not the case.

But on several nights I laid down hungry with nothing to taste.

And you had the life that closest resembled the Huxtables.

And me looked down upon, a burden, only a tax-deductible.

So why is it that when I get the long awaited appreciation I deserve.

Their smiles of pleasure and support strike such a nerve.

When I was counted out long before I entered the race.

As I re-enter the game and stand taking my rightful place.

First-born, oldest son the grandchild that began a new generation.

Consider this, ponder on it, let it penetrate, intellectual marination.

I can never be who you are and you can never be I.

But know that my successes came after several failed tries.

As I look at my existence some shade inevitably falls my way.

My mom half-heartedly cares; cancer took daddy away.

Your family blood flows at every function, my DNA shared by only a few.

Yet it appears that I'm more valued than you?

This truth supercedes all feelings and perceptions as it's a universal reality.

They are your real family and you're only sharing them with me.

When Your Sexy is Out of Season

48 degrees, walking your dog in a tank top.
Trying to be cute, girl you need to stop.
Daisy dukes with cowboy boots.
Ok on Miley Cyrus, but not on you.
A summer dress with spaghetti straps.
Sandals on and feet looking like crap.
Christmas just passed and it's days into the new year.
People are still brimming, full of holiday cheer.
And you eager to jump five months down the line.
Understand, a seasonal change will occur in due time.
But for now, put on your puff coat and sweater too.
A scarf for your neck, people are still getting swine flu.
Ear muffs, flannel, boots and long-sleeved button ups.
Wait on the skorts, capris and to roll your jean cuffs.
Legs exposed now can equate an eminent death or illness onset.
The roads are covered in snow or black iced, slippery and wet.
Heaters run all day and throughout most nights.
Be sure that skirt is accompanied with thick tights.
Fashion faux pas, and fashion mishaps.
It's winter, no tanks allowed with thin straps.
I know well the desire to show and share skin.
Wearing summer appeared is okay when that's the season we're in.
Cold weather outfits assembled can be a task and a treat.
Find a trench, collar shirt and heeled boots for your feet.
A trendy bag, nice belt and necklaces add to most looks.
An acquired skill, yes, but the answer lies in most books.
Magazines, the Fashion Network can sprinkle you with game.
Know that out of season looks just make you look lame.
Or you appear desperate and trying too hard to be seen.
A barrel of red apples and you sour and all green.
Somewhere along the way you lost it but Justin got it on track.
Please wait 'til its hot to show off your sexy back.

Life's a Comprehensive Exam

It's a trip that my school required comprehensive exam,
Paralled a journey I was experiencing, questioning my life and who I am.
Psychodynamic theory leads me directly to Dr. Sigmund Freud.
The question to answers never spoken an empty void.
The id, ego, superego and the beloved unconsciousness.
My mom, my kids, employment status, mortgage, an endless list.
A phallic symbol or the latency developmental stage.
Scared, angry, worried, happy, joyous, delirious rage.
Anxiety and a heightened sensitivity to the economic recession.
Tapping every resource—feng shui, trees, healthy diet to address my depression.
My primal quest of id guided food and sexual gratification.
Will empower my ego to attain what my ego ideal aspires—graduation.
My external reality waged war on my internal desire to matriculate.
An ongoing battle, unconscious and conscious, who wins? I can only speculate.
The structural conflict in place summons what little energy remains.
To live to the fullest, parent, pay bills, finish school—the desire to maintain.
The anxiety of an over achiever dining a' la carte, my cup runneth over.
To pull this off my dream, Irish luck, leprechauns and four leaf clovers.
Addressing wrongs done to me when I knew not what they were.
Seeking a corrective experience to repair the damages to me as extended by her.
Wishing to let down my guard and take on my many defenses.
Relinquishing my inner demons, anxiety all stressors and apprehensions.

Ten Bodies, One Soul—
the Remix

To my beautiful Sands, look what we have become.
Bodies of ten and a soul of one.
Headed towards greatness the journey's begun.
To success, wealth, power, prosperity; it all will come.
A team full of starters, we stand at the front of the line.
Too intelligent, too busy to waste any time.
With appointments and obligations to meet.
Walking swiftly with four inch stilettos on our feet.
To be the part, we must play the role.
Conquering and mastering everything our eventual goal.
Because for us it's pointless running full speed.
If we are not running and taking the lead.
So as we push forward through the rate race of life.
Encountering haters, obstacles and all of life's strife.
Our inner strength will guide us through the unforeseen.
And if we have trouble on one another we can lean.
Through all highs and lows the joys and the pain.
We've established a bond that will always remain.
To my sorors, my sisters, my sands, and my friends.
An eternal kinship has formed and will never end.
A plethora of talents an outpouring of skills in the bowl.
Yet remaining forever ten bodies and one soul.

You Can Survive

You can get over a bad childhood all you have to do is survive it.
    Determine your direction and destiny.
Repackage the bad and keep all the lessons learned,
    Thrive from it, Kaiser Permanente.
Lamenting over the past serves only to hold you victim,
    to yesterday's rainstorm.
Allow the sunlight to produce a rainbow,
    And from the rays stand in its warmth.
A broken heart, a lost love or bidding farewell,
    to your mom or your dad.
A good day never repeated,
    reminiscing about a joyful experience once had.
Bad days happen, but with perseverance,
    Character strength and faith you can overcome.
Welcome help from others but learn to stand strong.
    Be an army of one.
From the depths of your soul exists a will to live,
    Even when between a rock and a hard place.
Gotta bite the bullet, eyes focused.
    Maintain that serious, all business face.

Miranda's Rebuttal

My how the time has gone from 18 to 30;
    the years flashed by with lightening speed.
We started out kickin' it,
    partying with boys and smoking trees.
And even our nuptials occurred around the same bend,
    just a year apart.
But the things that we shared are changing and now what was,
    is a different new start.
You divorced your significant other,
    left with an empty womb.
And the death of that perception now
    what lies inside is an empty tomb.
My children came and blessed my existence
    to depths we can not share.
To equate life's purpose without having a legacy
    is something to difficult to compare.
And now your resistance to acknowledge happiness
    in all its varying degrees and shades.
Appears to be a passive resistance of envy,
    longing, disdain, jealousy and rage.
To say your hating and minimize my accomplishments
    as burdens which prevent me from outings.
Has me questioning your motives, our friendship.
    Yes know this I am doubting.
Being Samantha to my Miranda
    and speaking negatively of family life is shitty.
A bad episode, script misprint,
    the unedited version of Sex and the City.
I try to keep our friendship ties strong
    despite all of life's highs and lows.
But your developing disdain for children,
    a full balanced life is a devastating blow.

To our friendship and platform that you were placed
    as my bestie—my friend.
Still I wish you good luck in all your endeavors
    and in finding happiness in the end.
So if parting ways momentarily will grant you time
    to live the single life.
And develop a greater perspective,
    Of the blessings of being a mother and wife.
Just know that invites to outings
    but not being able to go due to the kids.
Does not always equate that my children are cock blocking the
    fun or interfering on the biz.
Because while sipping wine,
    talking and philosophizing about life is fun and needed
periodically.
Being in the company of my kids, listening to their voices
    and playing games is where I want to be.
Samantha the love remains even as our interest change,
    grow and we transition life's station.
Don't view my kids as barriers to fun and partying,
    for me that train has left the station.
We can hook up for drinks on an evening that
    childcare has been solidified.
And I encourage you to share your happy moments,
    just don't frown or look down on mine.

Hey, Little Sistah

Hey little sistah, life for you and me will not come with ease.
Not much smooth sailing there's no sea breeze.
To guide our course and direct us through.
For ourselves we must depend, that's what we must do.
No pale face privilege can we rely.
And if at first we don't succeed, again we must try.
But do not fret, for everyone experiences lows.
We just have to work harder to attain our goals.
Our hood tactics we must refine
While keeping it real, and in mind.
That black is beautiful, though only skin deep.
Our true inner treasure is what's beneath.
We have a legacy that dates back to royalty.
That explains our pride and dignity.
To come from greatness, we know our worth.
A treasure, priceless, is how we emerge from birth.
So keep it in mind when life's crap get's you down.
Remember your strength, rely on it when no one's around.
For life will demand you to stand or fall.
Cower to others, or stand up tall.
Head up, or head down on you it depends.
Regardless of how others view you it's determined by the lense.
That you view yourself and what you have to give.
Just give it your all, for you only have one life to live.
And though for us life's no crystal stair.
Remember, God will never give you anything you can not bare.

The First One

That first opens up your heart,
    To depths previously unknown.
A love unparallel to any other,
    An oasis, the parenting lane zone.
The look of their face
    So soft and serene.
Tiny hands, fingers and toes,
    An awesome, beautiful scene.
Who knew that love could capture and suspend my heart,
    To love this much it hurts.
I love you more than any aspect of life.
    Eagerly waiting for growth spurts.
To experience the remainder of my life
    As your mommy is a blessing.
That God bestowed upon me,
    My own living, breathing piece of Heaven.
And even as your grow,
    And lessons you continue to learn.
I learn and grow with you,
    And every stripe look forward to earn.
I knew from the moment I found out about your arrival,
    I loved you so.
But the extent, and that it would exist
    Throughout every part of my existence, that I did not know.
The selfish ways previously deeply embedded
    In my psyche have disappeared.
And now your well-being,
    Health, safety is my greatest care.
To love like this runs the gamet
    And every spectrum of emotion.
And the day you were born,
    to you I bid an eternal commitment and devotion.

Your smile warms my heart, tickels my soul,
>And brings tears to my eyes.
I love you more daily,
>And this happens without even a try.
My baby, my love, my first born,
>My cutie and honey bun.
Thank God for you, for opening my heart,
>For being my first one.

A Sweet Sleeping Symphony

Every night I listen to a sweet melody a symphony.
With altering tempo's, beats and up and down rhythms.
A duet with two sleeping participants,
Sometimes on one accord, sometimes with various solo's.
One taking the higher octave, the other on a lower, slower note.
I never listened to this or could hear this song before
God bestowed upon me a second and third ear.
Not until my capacity to love and live for love
Was I able to hear this glorious song.
Because of my blessings, two in fact
I can hear at a higher octave.
I can love at this same elevated rhythm as well.

I Can't Do Nothing For You Man

When I say I have no money,
People think I'm running drag.
Because I am a super fly diva
With a name brand handbag.
My money is so funny,
it's a comedian telling jokes.
Please do not be deceived
because I look this good being broke.
Yeah my clothes match
And appear to be new.
Delicate, cold water wash.
I know how to make it do.
My closet is lined with heels I brought
In early 2005.
When my funds were not condensed and on bills
I did have to divide.
No tuition cost, mortgage,
Or car payment to pay.
Just the spoils of being spoiled
In stores I would play.
Charging it to the game,
Buying my American dream.
Never having to spend on life's essentials
Is what it seemed.
Fast forward to today
As the year comes to an end.
No more lavish shopping excursions
No longer frivolous on what I spend.
Fighting to keep the roof over my head
And maintain the deed to my home.
An endless pit of debt
And past dues I'm striving to overcome.

So pardon me when I correct your incorrect
Assumptions about my duckets.
I'm several days late, a dollar short.
Can't take the stress, fuck it.
Know that my last season boots are in quick sand
And sinking fast.
So my effort is pulling my own boot strap
And saving my own ass.
Appearances can be deceptive
When judging a book by its cover.
So vacate my surroundings;
My finances, please do not hover.
The limits are real and if pushed
It's just for me and mine.
Working like a big dog,
Out here on a real money grind.
I'm praying for improvements
Requesting blessings for us both.
But I ain't got it
So please get off my pretty ass petty coat.

A Queen With My Thrown On Layaway

I laugh out loud but being short on change is the pits.
Compliments on purchased five years ago outfits.
Shoes with worn out heels made of faux snake skin.
Pair them with that shirt and jeans, and get more compliments again.
Jewelry that grandma bought when I was too young to drive and drink.
Yet when looked at, "she's got it made" is what you think.
My girls super shine, wearing designer jeans by the dozens.
But you didn't know they are hand-me downs, courtesy of their cousins.
PG&E got turned off and we stand around here in the dark.
Outward appearances, t's crossed, I's dotted—I'm on the mark.
The purses purchased four fashion seasons ago reel in much attention.
Past due bills, liens, foreclosure sale—did I mention?
My heels are in need of a professionals expertise and care.
I do them myself; can't afford a pedicure.
And as I faux fix my toe tips and arch my brows with a tweezer.
I wait to exhale, time-out. I need a financial breather.
It's evident royalty need not sit on a throne to command respect.
This queen is living from overdraft charges, insufficient funds and past due checks.

Head held high above the clouds, the bullshit and petty non-essentials.

Trying to clothe, house and feed my kids without losing it and going mental.

Life necessitates that I lose pounds and return to pre-baby me.

Can't afford to purchase any new items; we don't have no money.

Saying my prayers and working hard to reach my goals.

Will reach the other side of the bridge, now just paying my toll.

Bail Me Out

Damn, what's a sistah to do,
when work and life stress are coming down and closing in.
Taught to go to school, work hard
And for what, an inevitable end.
Struggling as is to help my family
With my husband dragging his feet.
And now here I stand, a rider
Facing emment defeat.
Take two steps forward
And get pushed back four.
Giving all of myself
What's left, nothing more.
I'm tired and worn thin
By the list of obligations.
Want to live by words
And submit my work resignation.
To give as much
With so little recognition.
Firing my gun,
But quickly running out of ammunition.
The backs of the strong
do ultimately bend and brake.
And for what?
Unemployment, low wages, reduced pay rate.
People look hard
but never truly see me.
And when I snap back
They act so stupidly.
I'm human, I cry
My tears leave wet trails.
Want to pull out my hair.
And bite off all my nails.

Eager for some relief or aid
But not a likely outcome.
Like a Katrina victim praying for help,
doing it without them.
Stress and anxious nerves
Compromising my physical health.
Job uncertainties, life crossroads
Interfering with my wealth.
Too old for school, need to be a teacher
And receive pay.
For the lived knowledge that I've
Acquired along the way.
Agoraphobia, claustrophobia, unemployment phobia
Walls drawing in.
Please God or Obama bail me out
And make the worries come to an end.

Thanks

It's interesting how in life we are not encouraged to pay homeage
to people whom we admire and respect.
Instead we are so focused on getting ours and working like slaves
to earn our next check.
But when the feeling presents itself to express to someone
How their actions have influenced you.
We stumble on words, become too busy with 'more important'
matters and act like we forget how to.
When you are surrounded by movers and shakers to stand still
And exhale may cause you to lose the lead.
But in a single man race you'll win no matter
How quickly you run; you determine the speed.
So take the time to enjoy where you are
And reflect on your point of origination.
Should in fact be a healing experience a happy cry
An opportunity at elated jubilation.
Allowing the drive of someone else to prompt movement
On your part is healing for the soul.
To take a step and then start running in that direction
To attain and achieve your goals.
Sometimes we move out of force
Are pushed or have our backs shoved against a wall.
Instead of lamenting about it, be glad you got gas
And that your vehicle is no longer stalled.
Other times it's the nay-sayers
Doubters and haters that provide that final boost.
Regardless you are moving, running faster
Than Oranthal—the juice is loose.

So I'm going to take this time to pay my honest gratitude
And sincerest thanks.
To everyone, believer, friend or foe
Who has encouraged me to climb up the ranks.
Thanks for being a trail blazer
Motivator and star in your own creative, outstanding way.
Thank you for providing me guidance, examples of what and
what not to do
And sending me on my way.

Swept Away

It never ceases to amaze, even though it should, how simple and selfish people are.
Out for self above all else, no matter the cost or sacrifice, to those less fortunate souls.
While you're grinning from ear to ear about your most recent purchase and acquisition.
Someone else is struggling to eat, provide shelter for their children and clothe their backs.
To their sorrows you turn a blind eye and drift off into your world of empty possessions and spiritless artifacts.
To give a second thought becomes too large a task.
Instead of offering a helping hand,
You'd rather take that hand and the other one, moved by two feet, and get French tips and bogus designs.
No one is asking you to swim for them, but from your yacht can you at least toss a life saver this way.
But that too becomes too much of an effort; you hope for a speedy death drowning into a broken, empty existence.
For if underwater, drifting away, my pain and suffering is never acknowledged and you are free to carry on the same.
But as the broke man drifts away to eternal nothingness, your position falters one notch.
You see, to stand above the rest requires the rest to be around
And for them to reside at your heels.
When the rug floats from under your feet, your bare pedicured toes are exposed and rest on the sand.
And once you land, falling from your comfortable elevated, seemingly untouchable position from the ground.
Falling again and faltering once more does not resemble the far off unimaginable scene of your mind's movie reel.

Look down and then look all around and you realize no one is down on this level but you, fright and fear set in.

Yelling for help and watching the yacht you once owned sailing away and no one concerned with throwing you a life raft.

This unsettling feeling begins to eat away at you and your untouchable spirit is being consumed by uncertain certainty. You know how it ends and before you can close your eyes and take one last breath

You too are swept away.

And the yacht party continues waiting for the next pedicured foot To touch down.

The Deception of
Perceived Strength

Is it because I'm built like a brick house
That you believe I can carry your load?
Is it because I'm a home owner that you believe
I'm obligated to invite you into my humble aboad?
Is it because my shirt matches my slacks, my heels
And my handbag coordinates with impeccable fashion taste.
That you believe I have money to pop bottles,
Going one endless shopping sprees—money to waste?
Is it because my laugh radiates the room, ricochets off walls
And permeates even the loudest crowd
That you take my joy for granted and expect me
To walk around with my head held low and bowed?
Is it because my arm's look like First Lady Michelle's
That you believe I am able to support you?
Do you think my rest breaks in between busy days, chores and
sleepless nights, mean I have nothing to do?
Is it because my confidence, outward expressions of poise and
control
Have significantly influenced my presentation and stance?
That you feel I should do more, give more
And perform because you've given me a chance?
Do you have the capacity to recognize the limits of one's strength
when their actions serve to deceive?
Please get off my back, stop placing unrealistic demands
And just be happy with what I give and what you receive.

Thee Is Me

One day I died and arrived in Heaven. There I saw my loved ones from yester year who departed from Earth before me. There was my daddy, his daddy and a host of cousins, aunts and uncles. After rejoicing in their presence, I turned and looked for God. My daddy knew what I wanted and he directed me down a hallway with the instructions, "at the end turn right".

I followed my daddy's directions and at its end, I turned right. There I came to a door and decided to open it.

When I opened the door, I was in a room filled with mirrors. My reflection peered back at me from all directions. Being an admire of myself, I smiled outward and that same smile was sent back to me many times over.

After gloating in the essence of me for sometime, I began to question out loud, "where is God? I really want to meet Him".

All the me's in the room, with the exception of one asked that question with me.

But that one me who remained silent initially, spoke out.

In my own voice with moves and mannerisms of mine I replied,

I am God. I am the God in you. You see, on Earth I could only speak to you through a Book, the Good Book. But as you stand before me today, I stand before you. I am the God within and only since your arrival to Heaven can you see an outward physical manifestation of me. I was with you during all your trials and tribulations. And since your soul and the souls of the departed are what exists in Heaven, I no longer have to remain concealed in your inner being. You see, because what was hidden within is all that is out, that matter and that exist here in my kingdom. I made you in my image. And my image, as I looked on you during your creation is the image you see of yourself today. Welcome home. You are now me and we is with thee and thee is me.

The World As We Know It

Sometimes it seems like the Earth is taking herself back.
Animals threatening and harming joggers,
Undomesticated predators ready to attack.
Wild turkeys running up and around
The lane.
It's crazy, sexy, their cool
Fucking insane.
Deer roaming at night
And wolves out on the prowl.
Inevitably, unfortunately for someone
It's going down.
Fire season extends for
Most of the year.
Snow storms for three months
And then fire season's back here.
Cliffs are literary
Crumbling around.
In a moments notice,
The seaside will be falling down.
Fires, storms, and the ice caps
Are melting away.
Mandatory now to wear sun block
Every day.
Skin cancer shines downs
With rays from the sun.
Toxins seep into the ozone
From Chevron, Shell, Exxon.
The natives instructed to handle Her
With caution and care.
Disrespectful to the gift from our Father
Of losing it we don't scare.
When his angels descend

One at a time.
In stages we'll meet
His presence—glorious and divine.
Storms occur frequent but will not be
A final bow.
But soon it will happen, if we do not figure out
What and then how.
Like how movies depict the end of the human race
Will soon manifest.
But not by vampires, New Moon's cast
Biting you right above the chest.
The end will resemble the beginning
But just in reverse.
The evolutionary upswing signifies
That we are really off course.
Where every hierarchy will fall
To its knee.
What and who were at the top will fall
To levels below that of the sea.
Animals over mankind,
Standing at the top of the stepple.
Wolves, bobcats, turkeys
Attacking and killing people.
Volcanoes erupt after decades free
Of heat, lava and ash.
Massive bug sprayings, sun allergies
Asthma creating a rash.
Rationing water use, limiting fire burning
And spare the air days.
Choose your poison, the world as we know it
Is fading away.
So think before you breath
And with every exhale.
Know that she has tired from our failures
And is bidding this sorrow farewell.

An anointed spirit will carry us
From this world threw the Pearly Gates of Heaven.
After massive world devastation
Occurs from the angels, all seven.
Be weary of people
And paw foot predators too.
Anyone and everything can attack now days
And ultimately pose a threat to you.

Vixen

Men have always loved me
Swarm around me like a hive of honey bees.
More like I'm queen bee
And they want a taste of me.
It's not a secret or surprise.
Go ahead, take a look
Deep into my eyes.
Beware, not to get lost
With a glance.
As my eyes twinkle
And dance.
Multi-dimensional,
You want the layers to unfold.
Oh, no! Slow your roll.
Searching like a miner to find my gold.
Sailing like a pirate
To sink a ship.
Mesmerized by my talk, by my mouth,
By my lips.
Engulfed by my presence
And confident stance.
Your mind churning,
Thinking of ways to spark a romance.
Wanting to hold my hand.
Being eager to start
With the opportunity of having
Even a small fraction of my heart.
But me, I'm one who loves
Hard and fast.
You ultimately become
A thing of the past.

A memory, a smile
A reminent of last week.
The one that did that;
My archived super freak.
I don't fault you
Or cast any blame.
For if I were you,
I'd love me just the same.
My walk stops men
Dead in their tracks.
And when I pass,
They feel compelled to look back.
My sense of style is a step
Above the rest.
Fashionable and trendsetting
At its best.
Indy 500 my curves
Are more fatal and defined.
From my breast, down my back
My hips and behind.
The nape of my neck
To my pinkie toe.
Up my leg, to my thigh
Caressing my elbow.
The bottom of my feet
And the palm of my hand.
Erotic, erotica
I captured the heart of another man.
Like a predator
Ready leaning in for the kill.
I give love
And seize hearts at will.
What is this formula,
You ask what I'm mixin'.
Hot chocolate, intelligence and sex appeal.
The recipe of a vixen.

Fear

I fear you
You awaken feelings in me
That are completely foreign.
Never before have I played
Such a deadly venomous game of roulette.
Handling a double edge sword
You cut me.
Deep, hard and long.
I excite at your touch.
The thought of those sensual lips
Against my skin.
Your hands all over my body
I'm your slain prey
And you my predator.
I've been seized.
Your soul has engulfed mine.
And now I succumb to you.
We danced a twisted tango
And you swept me away.
You extended a rose
I accepted.
And the thorns pierced my skin.
In the same fashion you pierced my heart.
But I was too engulfed in you.
And this torrid rapture of lust
To even notice the blood stained cloth above my chest.
Crimson rain drops soil my feet.
Instead of patting myself and compressing the leak until it
stopped.
You smothered me in your arms.
And I forgot about the pain you enduced.
Instead I enjoyed you for comforting me.

I melted in your company
And desperately tried to intertwine.
My oozing chocolate
With your gushing vanilla
A combination so sweet.
But it was bittersweet
A semi-sweet combination
That proved satisfactory but not truly rewarding.
Each galiant attempt to mix you in me
Was admirable but this secret recipe
Lacked a main ingredient.
It was not your eyes or gentle touch.
Nor was it my unquenchable desire for you.
It was the fear of knowledge.
You knowing me;
Me knowing you
And them knowing us?
This perplexing situation questions every moral instilled in love.
How can love exist when I fear you?

. . . But I'm Taken

Speaking to you, my long lost friend
Was so nice.
Me updating you about my husband
You sharing about your wife.
Behind the pleasant convo
I picked up on the old feelings.
When we were a pair
And to me your love you were dealing.
That subtle smile
That remained planted on my face.
When you nibbled here
And how good your lips taste.
My thoughts to were flying
To the good ole' days of yesteryear.
When onto me and me onto you
Together or always near.
The couple that was voted to make it
Beyond the teens.
A possibility to us,
So young but from what it seemed
We were destine to marry
After years of seperation.
This run in was kizmit
And possibly a fateful invitation.
To experience each other
Not as teens but much older
To love again and to provide
Whenever a supportive shoulder.
But to travel down a road
We have already paved.

Is like starting over,
Gunning to win a game just played.
And even as I remember the passion
Every time we speak.
Or better still, I can recall
You elevating my internal body heat.
Those lips, your hands ravaging me
All over and everywhere.
But in the past we both must
Leave the memories there.
But for the record
Please don't get my words mistaken.
If time and opportunity were right,
I'd be yours again,... but I'm taken.

My Repetoire and Your Influence

It'a a shame we didn't go
Out with a bang.
Your body had me and I loved
The hang of everything.
I wanted to give you fireworks
Like the fourth of July.
Exploding with orgasmic eruptions
On a sex induced high.
But our love affair plateaud
Shortly after May.
When April showers brought rain
And stormy weather our way.
Initially it was cute our romance
Marched to a different beat.
But who could predict
That would result in romance defeat.
I wanted so many more possibilities
At being with you.
In every physical area
You knew exactly what to do.
At least 20 more times
I wanted to create that experience.
That electric attraction and symbiotic
Consumation with you I miss.
Our connection permeated deep
To my neuronal soul.
My body, my heart
And my being you stole.
To question the what if's
And reflect with regret.
Is to totally over look
And ignore what I did get.

You are forever etched in my mind,
Heart and parts and places to delicate to say.
Your presence influenced my existence
From our first kiss to today.
So thank you for the love, lovin'
And all the one on one instruction.
You have influenced my secret talents
And love making repetoire construction.

Why Didn't We . . .

Why didn't we move beyond that first kiss?
I feel it was an opportunity missed.
Circumstances as they may.
You were unattainable and me in the same way.
Your warm embrace and my gentle touch.
Undeniable, mutual lust.
I catch myself fantasizing on what could be.
Me on top and you inside me.
I visualize your touch ever so slight.
Romantic, Shakespear; A midsummer's night.
On the shores of Kaui'i
On the dock of The Bay
On your momma's couch
Janet Jackson-anytime, any how, any way.
But a last that opportunity never did manifest.
Standing by wanting with panting chest.
Now years have passed but yet I remain perplexed
Because I really want to know,
Why didn't we . . . have sex?

Made in the USA
Las Vegas, NV
15 November 2020